31 DAYS
TO BUILDING
A MARRIAGE
THAT WILL LAST

MARRIED FOR GOOD

DAVID FAUST

HEART SPRING PUBLISHING · JOPLIN, MISSOURI

To my wife, Candy

Special thanks

to *Jim Eichenberger*, who first invited me to write a devotional guide
for engaged couples, and to *Dick Alexander* for allowing me to adapt
his idea for the TALK acrostic which appears at the end of each chapter.

International Standard Book Number 0-89900-911-5

Thirty-one Days to Building a Marriage That Will Last

Day

1

~❧ Day 1 ❧~

MARRIAGE FROM THE INSIDE OUT

*W*hen my wife and I became engaged, my future father-in-law made us an offer. "I'll give you $100 and a ladder," he joked, "if you'll just elope and keep me from having to go through all the hassle of a wedding!"

He was only kidding, but as our wedding approached, I began to understand what he meant. For all the joy it brings when two people get married, a wedding also involves countless details.

There are dresses to buy and tuxes to rent, invitations to print and mail, and rings to select and size. The engaged couple needs to talk with a minister, a florist, a musician or two, a photographer, and perhaps a videographer. There's food to prepare, a cake to decorate, and a marriage license to secure. The final days leading up to the wedding are a blur of activity—the rehearsal, the ceremony, the reception, the gifts, the honeymoon.

Somewhere in the midst of the premarital mayhem there needs to be a quiet time. A time to reflect and talk quietly with God. A time to be thankful, and to prayerfully prepare for one of the biggest days in your life.

For when all the vows have been spoken, the gifts have been opened, the clothes have been packed away and returned to the Rent-a-Tux store, and the last crumb of wedding cake has been washed down with a cup of punch, two people have a life to build together. And all the decorations in the world won't matter if there isn't peace in their hearts.

God builds strong marriages from the inside out. Over these thirty-one days, put the hassles aside and take time to focus on the quiet, inner side of what marriage is all about.

Open your heart to God and his love.

*Take the time to **TALK** about this topic on the next page.*

Thank God—"Thank you for providing inner peace in the midst of this busy time as we plan our wedding."

Ask God—"God, in the flurry of all the details, help us not to overlook the spiritual dimension of our relationship with each other and with you."

Listen to God—"Man looks at the outward appearance, but the Lord looks at the heart" (1 Sam. 16:7b).

Know more about what God wants you to do—There are several things you can do to nurture the spiritual side of your relationship. Arrange with a minister or a counselor to spend time in premarital counseling. Pray that God will help you build a healthy marriage. Talk with a happily married couple you respect, and ask for their input.

Day

2

⚜ Day 2 ⚜

THE HONEYMOON

You know the honeymoon is over when . . .

* ⚜ It no longer sounds strange to be called "Mr. and Mrs."
* ⚜ Your wedding rings lose that unfamiliar feel.
* ⚜ Your friends finally stop asking, "So how's married life?"
* ⚜ You've settled once and for all the question of who sleeps on which side of the bed.

Long ago God prescribed a generous amount of time for newlyweds to enjoy each other and adjust to married life. "If a man has recently married, he must not be sent to war or have any other duty laid on him. For one year he is to be free to stay at home and bring happiness to the wife he has married" (Deut. 24:5). A whole year? That's a long honeymoon!

Anyone can be happy while enjoying a few days in a romantic hideaway. The real test comes during the first year of marriage as a couple starts to build lifelong habits of interaction. It's not unusual to experience some emotional ups and downs in the first year. You're trying to blend two households, and there's a lot to learn as you share everything from a bed and a bathroom to a bank account.

It's likely the term honeymoon originated when people compared married love to the stages of the moon as it waxes and wanes. The good news? Marriage doesn't have to go downhill after the honeymoon is over. Many couples find that their marriages get better with the passing of time. The bonds of love grow stronger as you pass through the initial adjustments and develop greater maturity as individuals and as a couple.

Newlyweds do have fun—but not all the fun. Why not commit yourself to have a healthy, growing relationship even when you're a couple of "oldlyweds"?

*Take the time to **TALK** about this topic on the next page.*

Thank God—"I am grateful, God, for the excitement this new chapter in my life holds for me and my spouse."

Ask God—"Show me how to help our marriage get off to a good start, not only on the wedding day and during the honeymoon, but throughout the first year of our life together."

Listen to God— "'For I know the plans I have for you,' declares the Lord, 'plans to prosper you and not to harm you, plans to give you hope and a future'" (Jer. 29:11).

Know more about what God wants you to do— What do you think your first year of married life will be like? Many couples put some of their wedding cake into the freezer so they can enjoy eating it together on their first anniversary. Write your spouse a note to be opened and read on your first anniversary while you enjoy your cake together.

Day

3

❧ Day 3 ❧
MY WIFE'S SUITCASE

*O*n our honeymoon I watched with mild amusement as my bride stuffed her belongings into an oversized olive green suitcase.

Now, I was already satisfied that my bride was the most beautiful woman on earth, so I didn't think she needed to carry along extra supplies to make her better looking. Plus, having grown up in a family of all boys where fashion meant buying a new pair of jeans, I didn't see much need for the amazing array of garments, toiletries, and cosmetics Candy insisted on bringing along. Every time I wrestled her heavy suitcase into the trunk of our car, I teased her about all the baggage she had brought into our marriage.

Then one day it hit me that I had some baggage of my own. Every married person does, actually. We all bring into our marriages an array of experiences from our pre-marriage days. What kind of relationship did we have with our parents and siblings? What about previous dating experiences or engagements? Are we on the same wavelength spiritually, emotionally, socially, and financially? What kind of standard of living are we used to enjoying?

Are there some painful experiences from the past that we need to face and sort through before we marry?

My wife and I have passed our twenty-seventh wedding anniversary, yet we're finding that we still have a lot to learn about each other. We're glad that early in our relationship, we learned to talk honestly and openly about any baggage that would weigh us down.

And personally, I'm glad that we finally exchanged the olive green suitcase for a sleek new black one that rolls smoothly along on wheels.

Take the time to **TALK** *about this topic on the next page.*

Thank God—"I'm grateful for all the ways you have prepared my spouse and me to join together in marriage."

Ask God—"Help us to be honest with each other about any 'baggage' we're bringing into our marriage—and then to put the past behind us."

Listen to God—"Therefore, if anyone is in Christ, he is a new creation; the old has gone, the new has come!" (2 Cor. 5:17).

Know more about what God wants you to do—An objective third party can help you sort through the baggage of your past as you prepare for your future together. If you haven't already done so, why not call a church or a Christian counselor in your community to discuss premarriage counseling?

Day

4

❧ Day 4 ❧
I PROMISE

*M*ale-female relationships typically go through three stages.

First there are the "wows"—those exciting moments when you first meet, and you begin to picture yourselves together. Courtship is filled with "wows."

Then there are the "vows"—those solemn promises you make to each other on your wedding day. You stand before God and other witnesses, affirming your love and faithfulness.

But after the vows comes a third stage: the "nows." Most of marriage is lived in this third stage—making a living, paying the bills, handling the daily grind.

Successful couples find ways to weave some wows into the nows. They keep alive the wonder of it all and never lose the sense of awe they experienced when they first pledged their love. Through all the nows, successful couples are faithful to their vows. "For richer, for poorer, in sickness and in health" isn't a multiple choice test!

On your wedding day, you give your partner an incredible gift. You say, "I'll be there for you till the day one or both of us dies. Through all the 'nows,' I will keep my vows. You can count on me . . .

"I promise."

Thank God—"Thank you for the commitment my partner and I have made to each other, and for the security and stability our wedding vows represent."

Ask God—"Help each of us to be faithful to the promises we have made."

Listen to God—"Dear friends, since God so loved us, we also ought to love one another. No one has ever seen God; but if we love one other, God lives in us and his love is made complete in us" (1 John 4:11,12).

Know more about what God wants you to do— Love is a verb. It's more than just something we feel. It's also a choice we make and an action we take. Think about the promises you have made to your partner. With God's help, resolve that you will always be faithful to your wedding vows as long as you live.

Day

5

~ Day 5 ~

ANYHOW LOVE

*B*enjamin Franklin advised, "Keep your eyes wide open before marriage, half shut afterward."

It's smart to enter marriage with your eyes open. Be honest about yourself and about your partner. Have you talked frankly about each others' strengths and weaknesses? How do each of you react when you're tired or depressed? Do you communicate thoroughly about your values, goals, worries, and beliefs? Before you marry, you must face these questions with your "eyes wide open."

After you are married, you will continue to grow in your understanding of each other. But in Ben Franklin's words, that's when you'll need to keep your "eyes half shut." In other words, accept the things about each other that you cannot change.

A marriage counselor calls this "anyhow" love. It's the kind of love that says, "I don't agree with what you're saying, but I'll listen carefully anyhow." Or, "I don't understand why you feel that way, but I'll respect your opinion anyhow." Or, "Right now it doesn't appear that you're holding up your end of the bargain, but I'll fulfill my role in our marriage anyhow (and not resent you in the process)."

According to Victor Hugo, "The supreme happiness of life is the conviction of being loved for yourself, or more correctly, being loved in spite of yourself." You may not see eye-to-eye on every issue with your spouse. But you can learn when to keep your eyes wide open—and when to keep them half shut.

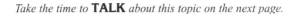

Take the time to **TALK** *about this topic on the next page.*

Thank God—"Thank you for the strengths I see in my partner."

Ask God—"Help me to be patient, kind, and forgiving when I see my partner's weaknesses."

Listen to God—"Be kind and compassionate to one another, forgiving each other, just as in Christ God forgave you" (Eph. 4:32).

Know more about what God wants you to do—Today, talk with your partner about "anyhow love." Discuss what it means to love each other in spite of your mutual imperfections.

Day

6

❧ Day 6 ❧

HAVING FUN
TOGETHER

*M*y wife thinks it's funny that I keep several joke books on the nightstand next to our bed. She'll be brushing her teeth when suddenly I burst into laughter as I read a funny Dave Barry story or a "top ten list" from one of my books.

Humor is a serious part of a healthy marriage. Sometimes funny things happen unplanned. My friend Bart owns a nervous Cocker Spaniel that gets frightened every year on the fourth of July because of all the fireworks. Last year the dog was already scared from the fireworks when a thunderstorm blew through the neighborhood, and the loud thunder added to the dog's terror. Half asleep, Bart dutifully arose from bed and led the dog outside for a brief visit to the doggy restroom— but in his sleepy state, my friend absentmindedly closed the back door of the house and heard it lock behind him. Until that moment, it was a minor detail that Bart was wearing only his underwear. Suddenly he was faced with leading his dog back to the front door of the house, where he stood in the rain ringing the doorbell until his wife arose to let Bart and the dog back inside!

Funny things happen—and get retold over and over, with greater embellishment, in families where joy is real and smiles are common. Why wait for the unplanned laughs? Build them into your regular time together. Rent funny videos. Play board games with friends who make you see the lighter side of life. Laugh together whenever you can.

You've heard the old saying, "He who laughs last, laughs best"? Here's another one: "The marriage filled with laughter lasts best."

Take the time to **TALK** *about this topic on the next page.*

Thank God—"Lord, I'm glad you've given me and my spouse so many reasons for joy! Thank you for the fun we have together."

Ask God—"Fill our home with wholesome fun, contagious good humor, and laughs that lighten our load."

Listen to God—"A cheerful heart is good medicine, but a crushed spirit dries up the bones" (Prov. 17:22).

Know more about what God wants you to do—Do you and your partner sometimes take yourselves and your relationship too seriously? Think about ways you can add more fun to your time together.

Day

7

❧ Day 7 ❧

POWER STRUGGLES

*N*ot long ago I spent a week on the Oregon coast, where I spoke for a conference at a nearby retreat center. My home for the week, which I shared with three other men, was a rustic cabin on a hill overlooking the Pacific Ocean.

Early one morning as I worked on my laptop computer, one of my housemates began to prepare breakfast. It was a beautiful setting: waves breaking against the rocks outside my window, the smells of coffee and toast wafting through the cool morning air.

Suddenly the lights went out. With a microwave oven, a coffee pot, electric lights, and a computer all competing for a limited amount of power, there simply wasn't enough to go around. It took us a while to find the circuit breaker and restore the lights—and then we had to adjust by reducing the demand for power. As I recall, I left my computer off for a while. (Coffee and toast took precedence!)

Too often, couples engage in power struggles. Their conversations degenerate into battles of the wills—and battles of the "won'ts"! Why can't she spend money the way she wants? Why can't he do whatever he wishes with his leisure time? Why is she so often late? Why is he so messy?

Real power isn't gained by getting your own way. In fact, sometimes the greatest power comes from giving in—by turning off your own part of the "power drain" and refusing to quarrel over minor issues. Mutual consideration goes a long way in any relationship—and it can keep a marriage running on full power.

Take the time to **TALK** *about this topic on the next page.*

Thank God—"Thank you, God, for the lessons you have taught me when I didn't get my own way."

Ask God—"Remind me that true greatness and power come from serving others, not from pushing people around. Help me to serve my partner in love."

Listen to God—"Do nothing out of selfish ambition or vain conceit" (Phil. 2:3). "Serve one another in love" (Gal. 5:13).

Know more about what God wants you to do—Consider how power struggles affect your relationship with your spouse. How can you serve your partner today?

Day

8

~❀ Day 8 ❀~

FOR RICHER, FOR POORER

*I*n an episode of the classic TV show *I Love Lucy* Lucille Ball decides to earn some extra money by getting a job in a candy factory. Her first day on the job, her boss positions her on an assembly line where her job is to wrap pieces of candy as they move along a conveyor belt. The problem is, the conveyor belt keeps moving faster and faster until Lucy can't keep up. Her hands flail away and she stuffs several pieces of candy into her mouth, but it's obvious she will never be able to keep up.

Like Lucy in the candy factory, many couples today are struggling to keep up. Finances are a common trouble spot in marriage. When times are tight, it puts pressure on a husband and wife when they have to do without some things and work extra hours to make ends meet. In more prosperous times, poor money management still can sink a couple into the quicksand of debt.

Are you starting your marriage with any major debts? How do each of you handle money? Are you impulsive or thrifty, carefree or cautious, stingy or generous? Are the two of you in agreement about buying on credit? Handling the checkbook? Budgeting? Saving? Discretionary spending? Have you discussed what you will give back to the Lord and the church?

Your wedding vows say, "Till death do us part," not "Till debt do us part." Don't let material possessions come between you. The love in a healthy marriage is a treasure money can't buy.

*Take the time to **TALK** about this topic on the next page.*

Thank God—"We enjoy many material blessings and physical comforts. Thank you for providing our needs and granting us many of our wants."

Ask God—"Help us to avoid the rat race. Enable us to guard against greed, get out (and stay out) of debt, and find joy and contentment in simple things. Never let money be a source of division between my spouse and me."

Listen to God—"For the love of money is a root of all kinds of evil. Some people, eager for money, have wandered from the faith and pierced themselves with many griefs" (1 Tim. 6:10).

Know more about what God wants you to do—Talk with your spouse about these common money myths: "Two can live as cheaply as one." "Buy now, pay later." "We want to have the same standard of living our parents enjoy right now—even though it took them many years to attain it."

Day

9

❦ Day 9 ❦

IN SICKNESS AND IN HEALTH

*O*n our wedding day in 1975, my bride gave me strict instructions about the wedding cake: "Don't try to stuff a big piece of cake into my mouth the way some grooms do!" I complied with her request, but only after teasing her for a moment by thrusting an enormous piece of cake in her direction. We still have a picture of that moment in our photo album, and after all these years the look on Candy's face still says, "Don't you dare!"

Awhile back, Candy and I visited our friend Russ while he fed his wife Marian at the assisted living center where she lives. Marian is suffering in an advanced stage of Alzheimer's disease. Spoonful by spoonful, Russ gently pushed a pureed ham and cheese sandwich toward this dear woman he married more than half a century ago.

Marian didn't speak. As Russ fed her, though, there was no mistaking the trust in her eyes.

Newlywed love sparkles with anticipation. Surrounded by festive decorations and smiling friends, the new bride and groom feast on wedding cake and dream about the future. But there's a kind of love seasoned by the years that's even sweeter in its own way. It's the love of a man and woman who said "in sickness and in health" and meant it—a love that survives scary surgeries and financial downturns, job changes and difficult moves, and monotonous periods when nothing seems to change at all.

It's the mature love of two people who have laughed and cried together, held hands in church, and shared their lives at a level newlyweds know nothing about. And when the time comes, it's the kind of love that gently spoons pureed ham and cheese into the quivering lips of a cherished partner.

The world could use a whole lot more of that kind of love—the kind that comes not by chance, but by choice.

*Take the time to **TALK** about this topic on the next page.*

Thank God—"You will give us the strength to handle any hardships life may bring."

Ask God—"Give us grace to face sickness and other painful circumstances with steadfast trust in you and unfading loyalty to each other."

Listen to God—"Praise be to the God and Father of our Lord Jesus Christ, the Father of compassion and the God of all comfort, who comforts us in all our troubles, so that we can comfort those in any trouble with the comfort we ourselves have received from God" (2 Cor. 1:3,4).

Know more about what God wants you to do— Think about the part of your wedding vows that pledges your loyalty "in sickness and in health." How do you think the two of you would handle a prolonged illness, an accident, or some other physical or emotional hardship? Are you cultivating a deep faith in God and a support network of encouraging friends who could assist you in times of physical need?

Day

10

Day 10

THE RIVER

"The river has never looked more beautiful than it does today," said the old man to his wife.

She nodded and smiled.

Oh, the river wasn't as wide as it would be farther downstream—or as deep. But for the last thirty years, the two of them had lived in a small white farm house on a grassy hill overlooking the river. And each morning, they peered out the kitchen window while he brewed the coffee and she made whole wheat toast.

They never grew tired of looking at the river. They liked the way it glistened in the summer sunlight. The way the reflection of orange and yellow leaves danced on the surface in October. The way the icy stream carved smooth snow sculptures along its banks in January. They even found curious pleasure in those unpredictable days when spring rains made the muddy stream overflow its banks.

A few miles upstream from the farmers' house, a small creek joined with another stream almost the same size. At the point where the two streams merged, there was some turbulence. Churning rapids marked the spot where the two creeks struggled to become one.

But they did.

"Yep. It's never looked more beautiful than it does today," said the farmer as he gazed out the window. "I even think it's deeper than it used to be."

His wife smiled and squeezed his hand. "Like the two of us," she said.

*Take the time to **TALK** about this topic on the next page.*

Thank God—"Thank you, God, for helping the two of us move closer together in our journey through life."

Ask God—"When turbulent times come, help us understand that you're there with us, leading us to grow deeper and stronger than we were before."

Listen to God—"So they are no longer two, but one. Therefore what God has joined together, let man not separate" (Matt. 19:6).

Know more about what God wants you to do—What steps do you need to take to grow deeper as an individual? As a couple?

Day

11

Day 11

I RESPECT YOU

*A*s the words *spectacles* and *spectator* suggest, at its root, the word *respect* literally means something like "to look again" or "to see again."

People we respect deserve a second look.

A baseball player had better respect the pitcher who's capable of whizzing a 95-mile-per-hour fastball past his chin.

An employee had better respect the boss who has the power to promote or fire her.

A wise student will respect a teacher who has the ability to pass along valuable knowledge.

But nowhere is respect more vital than in marriage. Like a guardrail along a mountain road, healthy respect creates a safe boundary that can only be disregarded at one's peril.

In marriage two people say to each other . . .

❊ "Because I hold you in high regard, I will not mistreat you or mislead you."

❊ "Because I honor you as a person of extraordinary value, uniquely created by God, I will resist any temptation to disrespect or devalue you."

✳ "Because I respect you for who you already are, not simply for what I want you to become, I will not try to force you to change."

✳ "Because I respect the integrity of our relationship, I will be honest with you and tell you the truth in all circumstances."

✳ "Because I know the power of words to convey honor or dishonor, I will speak positively about you in public and respectfully to you in private, even when we disagree."

A wise person would never marry someone he or she doesn't respect. But what a wonderful gift it is to look your beloved in the eye and say with sincerity, "I respect you."

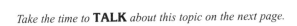

*Take the time to **TALK** about this topic on the next page.*

T_hank God_—"I'm glad to have a partner who is respectable."

A_sk God_—"Strengthen my resolve to treat my spouse with the honor he or she deserves."

L_isten to God_—"Each one of you also must love his wife as he loves himself, and the wife must respect her husband" (Eph. 5:33).

K_now more about what God wants you to do_—Are the two of you doing anything that tends to diminish your respect for each other? Think about how you could correct this. Today, tell your partner how much you respect him or her, and why.

Day

12

❧ **Day 12** ❧

LIVE AND LEARN

*W*hen my wife Candy was working the night shift as a nurse, I came home one evening to find her feeling worn out. After working three long nights in a row, she looked a bit bedraggled in her old tee-shirt and bluejeans when we set out for an evening walk.

As we walked along, she said, "Dave, I'm sorry I look like such a slob tonight." I shrugged and said, "That's okay."

Now, I thought I was being encouraging! Soon, though, Candy enlightened me that she would have preferred to hear me say something like this: "I love you, and you're beautiful to me no matter what."

We all live and learn—and after twenty-seven years, Candy and I find that we still have a lot to learn about each other. Couples enter marriage with different personalities, different backgrounds, different expectations, different levels of spiritual and emotional maturity. What happens when a "people person" marries a "private person"? Or an "outgoing, excitable" person marries an "introverted, thoughtful" person? What if the "big joker's" goofy sense of humor begins to get on his spouse's nerves? Or the "detail person" begins to drive her husband crazy because she's so obsessed with having everything a certain way?

What happens? We live and learn.

And accept and adjust and grow. And prepare to turn the page on yet another chapter in this adventure called marriage.

*Take the time to **TALK** about this topic on the next page.*

T*hank God*—"Marriage is an adventure. Thanks for all the things I'm going to learn through this experience."

A*sk God*—"Open my heart, God, to everything you want to teach me about my spouse and about myself."

L*isten to God*—"And this is my prayer: that your love may abound more and more in knowledge and depth of insight" (Phil. 1:9).

K*now more about what God wants you to do*—Today, think about one insight into your own personality that you could share with your mate in order to help him/her understand you better.

Day

13

Day 13

BEFORE THE SUN GOES DOWN

*Y*ears ago, radio commentator Paul Harvey told a story about a woman in a brand new Mercedes who was waiting for a car to back out of a parking space so she could pull in. But before she could do so, a young man in a Corvette convertible zipped around her and took the parking place. As she rolled down her window to complain, he yelled, "Sorry, lady. That's how it is when you're young and quick."

Wearing a determined frown, the woman immediately put her car in gear and smacked right into the back of the young fellow's Corvette. He screamed, "What do you think you're doing?"

And she replied calmly, "That's how it is when you're old and rich!"

Conflicts come in many forms, and it's amazing how petty and spiteful we can become when we don't handle them well. Marriages suffer when couples respond to conflict in unhealthy ways:

By drifting apart, withholding important facts or feelings for increasing lengths of time.

By engaging in hurtful name calling or frequent quarrels that are left unresolved.

By allowing their careers or hobbies to take them in completely different directions.

By developing close emotional bonds with opposite-sex confidants (which sow seeds for extramarital affairs).

By clinging to past hurts and allowing bitterness to poison their relationship.

The Bible says not to let the sun go down on your wrath. In other words, resolve conflicts on a day-to-day basis instead of harboring resentment in your heart. Communicate honestly about your differences, but do it with respect instead of blowing your spouse away with angry, destructive words. When you can't resolve conflicts on your own, seek wise counsel from advisors who will encourage your faith and support your desire to build a healthy marriage.

When conflicts come, stay positive and remember that your marriage can survive the storm with the Lord's help. Stay busy rowing, and you won't have time to rock the boat.

*Take the time to **TALK** about this topic on the next page.*

T*hank God*—"Thank you for being a God of peace, and for enabling us to face conflict without falling apart."

A*sk God*—"Help us to work out our differences each day instead of allowing old quarrels and lingering resentments to fester and damage our relationship."

L*isten to God*—"In your anger do not sin: Do not let the sun go down while you are still angry, and do not give the devil a foothold" (Eph. 4:26,27).

K*now more about what God wants you to do*— Unresolved conflicts put a heavy strain on a marriage. Have you and your mate developed effective ways to deal with conflicts quickly so they don't bog down your relationship?

Day

14

❧ Day 14 ❧
LISTEN UP!

A friend gave me a copy of a cartoon that showed a husband and wife lying in bed with a barbed wire fence stretching between them. The husband is saying to his miffed-looking bride, "Apparently I have done something to upset you."

Some of the biggest conflicts in marriage happen not because of angry words we say, but because of important messages we don't hear. Like people who have lived near an airport so long that they no longer notice the sound of the planes, we tune out the familiar voice of our mate.

Do you need to work on your listening skills? Does your body language tell your partner that you're offering your full attention? Do you maintain eye contact when he or she is talking? Do you avoid "competitive" conversations in which you're so busy trying to insert your own comments that you never grasp your partner's point of view?

There's only a small difference between *hear* and *heart*. If you aren't listening, you probably aren't loving.

Emotional intimacy doesn't happen when our conversations mainly consist of short, businesslike encounters or shallow, surface-level comments. Do you want more effective communication in your marriage? Listen up!

Thank God—"I'm glad to have a mate who listens to my feelings and thoughts—and who shares his/her inner self with me."

Ask God—"Please help me to really listen to my mate with empathy and sincere interest."

Listen to God—"Everyone should be quick to listen, slow to speak and slow to become angry" (Jas. 1:19).

Know more about what God wants you to do— Today, practice listening more intently to your mate. Try to say less and hear more.

Day

15

✤ Day 15 ✤
TENSE TIMES

*T*ension? It's what you feel when your flight leaves at 3:00, it's now 2:45, and you're stuck in traffic one mile from the airport.

It's what you feel when your favorite football team is behind by two points with five seconds to go as they line up to kick a 40-yard field goal.

It's the way you feel before a tough final exam.

It's the way you feel when the boss expects the same level of production even though he's cut your department's budget and workforce in half.

It's the way you feel when the photographer tells you your wedding pictures are going to cost more than you expected, your maid of honor shows up late for the wedding rehearsal, and you discover on the morning of the wedding that your burliest usher's tuxedo is a size 34 short—and the tux rental place is closed today.

Tense times come to every marriage. One person's exhausted, the other is feeling playful. One person is in a romantic mood, the other wants to be left alone. One person wants to have friends over for the evening, the other wants some privacy.

What eases the tension? Laughing together. Refusing to take yourselves too seriously. Being willing to

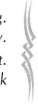

compromise. Praying for patience and understanding. Learning to live and love without getting your own way.

Tension? There's plenty around if you look for it. Peace? There's plenty of that available too—if you seek it from the hand of God.

Take the time to **TALK** *about this topic on the next page.*

Thank God—"Even in the midst of tense moments, you give me peace deep down in my soul."

Ask God—"Fill our relationship with contentment even during those times when we're tempted to let stress get the better of us."

Listen to God—"Let the peace of Christ rule in your hearts. . . . And be thankful" (Col. 3:15).

Know more about what God wants you to do—The Bible says, "Cast all your anxiety on him because he cares for you" (1 Pet. 5:7). What is the main source of tension you and your mate are facing right now? Offer it to God in prayer and ask him to fill you with peace.

Day

16

❧ Day 16 ❧
THE TROUBLE WITH US

$\mathcal{S}$omewhere I read why Adam and Eve got off to such a good start in their marriage: He didn't have to hear about all the men she could have married, and she didn't have to hear about the way his mother cooked!

Truth is, marriage isn't a 50-50 partnership. It requires 100% from each partner as we serve one another in love. The Bible says, "Wives, submit to your husbands, as is fitting in the Lord. Husbands, love your wives and do not be harsh with them" (Col. 3:18,19). The main point of this Scripture isn't to describe a chain of command; it's mainly talking about a circle of self-giving in which each spouse makes sacrifices for the sake of the other.

"Wives, submit." This doesn't mean a woman is inferior, that she's a doormat or a nonperson, or that her husband has a license to abuse her. It means she offers her husband respectful cooperation, appreciation, and admiration as he loves, leads, and leans on God for strength.

"Husbands, love." Another part of the Bible says it even more emphatically: "Love your wives just as Christ

loved the church and gave himself up for her" (Eph. 5:25).

A wise counselor says that from time to time every married person should remember to say, "The trouble with us is me." To love as Jesus loved requires sacrifice. Both partners must give 100%. Unselfishness is the essence of love—and the key to a strong and lasting marriage.

Take the time to **TALK** *about this topic on the next page.*

Thank God—"I appreciate the ways my mate gives up some of his/her preferences for my sake."

Ask God—"Help me to be unselfish, willing to go the extra mile for the sake of my mate."

Listen to God—"Be imitators of God, therefore, as dearly loved children and live a life of love, just as Christ loved us and gave himself up for us as a fragrant offering and sacrifice to God" (Eph. 5:1,2).

Know more about what God wants you to do— Identify one way you tend to act selfishly in your relationship with your spouse. Confess it to God, and ask him to help you act more lovingly and unselfishly.

Day

17

Day 17 ※

SOUL FOOD

*W*hen Candy and I were newlyweds she was an inexperienced cook, and I was—well, I was just a bad cook.

Her kitchen exploits included her first-ever apple pie, which looked a lot like a deflated football. Mine included what came to be known around our house as UFOs (Unidentified Frying Objects). In later years our children have been known to run in fright when I began making one of my "daddy casseroles" or my infamous bean soup. And our youngest daughter still complains about the time I volunteered to make her strawberry birthday cake—and it came out of the oven with the texture of an inch-thick slab of pink shoe leather.

A simple thing like eating together can be a challenge to a newly married couple. I like Mexican; Candy likes Chinese. I don't like eggs; she likes ketchup with hers. I like vanilla; she prefers chocolate.

Far more important is the kind of spiritual food a couple shares. What steps are you taking to nurture your faith? Do you and your spouse talk about spiritual things? Do you share a common worldview? Do you pray together? Are you developing friendships with people who will encourage your walk with the Lord? Are you part of a Bible study group?

As time goes by, you'll learn to adapt to each other's tastes in food. Meanwhile, your marriage will be greatly enriched if you'll also grow together in your walk with God. Jesus said, "Blessed are those who hunger and thirst for righteousness, for they will be filled" (Matt. 5:6).

*Take the time to **TALK** about this topic on the next page.*

Thank God—"Thank you, God, for hope and peace, and all the other spiritual blessings you have provided."

Ask God—"Lord, as our relationship with each other grows, help us also to develop our relationship with you."

Listen to God—"Like newborn babies, crave pure spiritual milk, so that by it you may grow up in your salvation, now that you have tasted that the Lord is good" (1 Pet. 2:2,3).

Know more about what God wants you to do— Today, think about the way you and your partner deal with faith issues. How could the two of you develop a deeper relationship with God?

Day

18

❧ **Day 18** ❧
I TRUST YOU

*L*ittle children trust their parents to feed and shelter them.

Banks hold money in trust for their depositors.

Restaurant diners trust their cooks to prepare their food safely and tastefully.

Airline travelers trust their pilots to navigate the planes safely toward their destinations.

Authors trust their editors.

Trust is an essential ingredient of everyday life. We have to extend trust, or we cannot function in a world that requires interaction with others.

Marriage is a supreme act of trust. In marriage two people say to each other:

* ❋ "Because I trust you to be faithful to me, I will not be jealous when we are apart."

* ❋ "Because I trust you to be honest with me, I will not doubt your words but accept them as the truth."

* ❋ "Because I trust that you don't want to hurt me, I will make myself vulnerable to you."

* ❋ "Because I trust that you'll never betray my

and feelings with you."

* "Because I know that love 'always protects,
always trusts, always hopes, always perseveres'
(1 Cor. 13:7), I will trust you with my emo-
tions, with my body, with my money, with my
secret self, with my future."

It would be foolish indeed to marry someone you
didn't completely trust. But what a great gift it is to look
into the eyes of your partner and say without hesitation,
"I trust you."

*Take the time to **TALK** about this topic on the next page.*

Thank God—"It's wonderful to have a partner I can rely upon to be faithful to me."

Ask God—"Never let anything weaken our trust in each other, God. Help us be faithful to our wedding vows and faithful to you."

Listen to God—"Trust in the LORD with all your heart and lean not on your own understanding; in all your ways acknowledge him, and he will make your paths straight" (Prov. 3:5,6).

Know more about what God wants you to do—In your relationship with your husband or wife, are either of you doing anything that weakens your trust in each other? Have you discussed this together? Find an opportunity today to tell your spouse how much you appreciate his or her trust-worthiness.

Day

19

Day 19

GAMES PEOPLE PLAY

*I*f you were to compare marriage to a sport or a game, what would it be? Marriage isn't a game; it's serious business. But that doesn't prevent married people from playing games with each other.

First there's the Dating Game, when you put your best foot forward and try to guess where your relationship is headed. Then there's the Newlywed Game, where you live in the glow of your happy new expectations, spend a lot of time in the bedroom, and begin to explore the many dimensions of matrimony. Unfortunately, for many couples, what follows next can be some other relationship games that are not so wonderful—like Tug of War, Aggravation, and Monopoly. Sadly, for some couples, married life can turn into one big War Game—and when that happens, nobody wins.

Healthy marriages include direct and positive communication, effective problem solving, conflict resolution, and lots of forgiveness.

When it comes to being truthful with your closest companion on earth, don't play games. When you do, even if you "win," you lose.

Thank God—"We don't have to deceive each other and play games with the truth in order to find acceptance. 'The truth will set us free.'"

Ask God—"Help us to be tactful yet truthful, honest yet honoring, tough but tender."

Listen to God—"Therefore each of you must put off falsehood and speak truthfully to his neighbor" (Eph. 4:25).

Know more about what God wants you to do—The manipulation, dishonesty, distrust, and bitterness that characterize marital "game-playing" have no part in a healthy marriage. Today, reflect on any "games" you and your partner have been playing with each other. Commit yourself to be real—and to build each other up instead of tearing each other down.

Day

20

~❧ Day 20 ❧~
COUPLES TO COPY

*J*ust as no two person's fingerprints are exactly the same, no two married couples are exactly alike. Each couple brings together a unique combination of personalities and gifts. Nevertheless, we can learn a lot from other couples whose marriages we admire.

For example, several married couples described in the Bible possessed some qualities worth imitating. Abraham and Sarah believed God's promises. Joseph and Mary obeyed God's instructions. Priscilla and Aquila worked together side by side and opened their home to others.

In my own experience, I've known several couples who inspire my wife and me to follow their example. Chuck and Annette inspire us to keep the spark of romance alive. Ray and Effie challenge us to live by faith. Paul and June motivate us to travel together and keep learning new things. Tom and Martha set a good example with their gracious hospitality. Jim and Carolyn have shown us how to persevere in serving God.

Do you know some couples who have happy marriages? Learn from their examples. They are living evidence that a great marriage is within your grasp.

T*hank God*—"Thank you for positive role models you've placed in our lives."

A*sk God*—"Help us set a good example for other couples who someday may imitate us."

L*isten to God*—"Remember your leaders, who spoke the word of God to you. Consider the outcome of their way of life and imitate their faith" (Heb. 13:7).

K*now more about what God wants you to do*—Think of a couple whose marriage you admire. Invite them out to dinner and ask them to tell you what marriage has been like for them.

Day

21

❖ Day 21 ❖
I LOVE YOU

*W*hat does it mean to say, "I love you"?

The ancient Greeks used several expressive words to capture different aspects of love.

Storge was the love of family relationship—the kind shared by brothers and sisters. It meant, "I love you because we share a common bond of kinship."

Philos was the love of friendship and brotherly kindness. It meant, "I love you because we share common interests and concerns."

Eros was the love of passion and romance. It meant, "I love you because you are attractive to me."

Agape was the love of decision, commitment, and self-sacrifice. It meant, "I love you because I consider you extremely valuable—so valuable that I'll do whatever it takes to act in your best interests."

A healthy, growing marriage includes love in all its dimensions. There's family loyalty, friendship, passion, and commitment. But a marriage thrives best when it's built on a foundation of *agape* love—the kind of sacrificial love that says, "I'll be there for you no matter what." *Agape* is the word the Bible uses when it says, "God is love" (1 John 4:16). It's the word used when Scripture says for husbands to "love your wives, just as Christ loved the church and gave himself up for her" (Eph. 5:25).

And it's the word used in the "love chapter" of the Bible, 1 Corinthians 13, which says, "Love is patient, love is kind. It does not envy, it does not boast, it is not proud. It is not rude, it is not self-seeking, it is not easily angered, it keeps no record of wrongs. Love does not delight in evil but rejoices with the truth. It always protects, always trusts, always hopes, always perseveres" (1 Cor. 13:4-7).

Take the time to **TALK** *about this topic on the next page.*

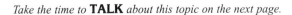

Thank God—"Our love is strong and growing."

Ask God—"Keep love alive in all its dimensions in our marriage. And help us, God, to build on the solid foundation of your love."

Listen to God—"And now these three remain: faith, hope and love. But the greatest of these is love" (1 Cor. 13:13).

Know more about what God wants you to do—Today, tell your mate, "I love you." Then using each of the four aspects of love described on p. 86, explain why you love him or her.

Day

22

❧ Day 22 ❧

PUT-DOWNS

*W*hen it comes to joking about marriage, comics know that the put-down will always get a laugh.

George Burns quipped, "I was married by a judge. I should have asked for a jury."

Rodney Dangerfield said, "My wife and I were happy for twenty years. Then we met."

Actually, though, most marriages could use some put-downs. Put down the newspaper so you can talk. Put down your defenses that keep you from opening up to your spouse. Put away the distractions that weaken the quality of your time together. Put away the TV remote control, get away from the computer, quit spending so much time at work, stop chipping away at your spouse's self-worth.

The Bible says, "Do not let any unwholesome talk come out of your mouths, but only what is helpful for building others up according to their needs, that it may benefit those who listen" (Eph. 4:29).

Most people need encouragement far more than they need another critic. And no one needs your encouragement more than your marriage partner.

Are you holding onto a grudge or a bad attitude that prevents you from encouraging your spouse? There's a simple solution. Don't hold onto it anymore. Put it down.

Take the time to **TALK** *about this topic on the next page.*

Thank God—"You have given us lots of positive things to build upon in our relationship. Thanks for the encouragement we derive from just being together."

Ask God—"Help us build each other up, not put each other down."

Listen to God—"But encourage one another daily . . . so that none of you may be hardened by sin's deceitfulness" (Heb. 3:13).

Know more about what God wants you to do—Evaluate the way you communicate with your partner. Are you the master of the put-down, or a steady source of encouragement?

Day

23

Day 23

IN-LAWS OR
OUTLAWS?

"Ken and I get along great most of the time," says Jennifer, "but it seems like every time we visit my parents, he ends up feeling annoyed and I'm depressed for days afterward."

Why do in-law relationships often become a source of conflict in marriage?

Some couples enter marriage naively, oblivious to the fact that they are embarking upon a lifelong relationship with their spouse's family as well as their spouse. Since it's hard to be truly objective about our own parents, some of us refuse to recognize our parents' shortcomings, while others magnify their faults. Add some personality clashes, spiritual and cultural differences, different socioeconomic levels, and some "unloosened apron strings," and you have a prescription for conflict—especially when holiday gatherings and social events compel relatives to spend time together whether they have much in common or not.

The Bible offers a balanced approach. A married couple needs to establish independence, for "a man will leave his father and mother and be united to his wife"

(Gen. 2:24). At the same time, a couple should practice inclusion of the extended family by honoring the in-
laws in appropriate ways, for the Bible also says, "Honor
your father and your mother" (Exod. 20:12).

Wise parents give their married children space, privacy, and room to grow. Wise married couples honor
their parents and cultivate with them a mature relationship based on friendship and mutual respect.

Take the time to **TALK** *about this topic on the next page.*

Thank God—"I appreciate the good qualities I see in our extended family."

Ask God—"Help us keep tension at a minimum with our in-laws. And help us to build a healthy home of our own while accepting our parents-in-law and including them in our lives in a way that shows appropriate honor and respect."

Listen to God—"But Ruth replied [to her mother-in-law, Naomi], '. . . Where you go I will go, and where you stay I will stay. Your people will be my people and your God my God'" (Ruth 1:16).

Know more about what God wants you to do—Today, ponder your relationship with your spouse's family. What could you do to strengthen the bonds with your in-laws?

Day

24

❧ Day 24 ❧
KEEPING WARM

*M*any a bride or groom discovers on the day of the wedding that his or her beloved has cold feet. Not a fear of getting married, mind you. This wonderful person literally has cold feet—which somehow end up planted firmly on the back of the mate's bare legs in the middle of the night!

I heard about one couple who couldn't agree on the right temperature for sleeping. He liked the room slightly cold with only a light sheet covering him while he slept. She, on the other hand, preferred to sleep in a warm room with heavy blankets piled on for further heat. Finally they thought they had resolved their problem when they bought an electric blanket with adjustable controls for each side of the bed. But through the night, they were both miserable. He was too hot, so he kept turning down the control. She was too cold, so she kept turning it up. In the morning they discovered their error: they had reversed the controls, so with each adjustment they only succeeded in making each other more miserable!

Like a glowing fire in a fireplace, married love needs regular attention. You have to stir the embers of romance, add some firewood by sharing fun and enrich-

ing new experiences, and fan the flames of love by sharing constant encouragement.

Don't let the fire go out. You need each other to
stay warm.

*Take the time to **TALK** about this topic on the next page.*

Thank God—"Lord, thank you for making my life warmer and more enjoyable by giving me a partner to share it with."

Ask God—"Help us to stick together and encourage one another day by day—and keep the fire of our love burning brightly."

Listen to God—"If one falls down, his friend can help him up. But pity the man who falls and has no one to help him up! Also, if two lie down together, they will keep warm. But how can one keep warm alone?" (Eccl. 4:10,11).

Know more about what God wants you to do—What tends to cool your devotion to your partner? Today, think about ways you can keep genuine warmth in your relationship.

Day

25

THE PHOTO ALBUM

"*D*o you want to see what I looked like as a little girl?" Susan asked as she pulled a well-worn photo album from the shelf in her parents' living room.

"Sure," nodded her fiancé, Rob. He settled next to Susan on the couch and put his arm around her shoulder.

"Here's a picture of me as a baby. Mom said I cried for an hour before Dad took it. See how red my eyes look?"

"What's this one?" Rob asked as he turned the page.

"That's me at age five—my first day of kindergarten. Every time I look at it, I still remember how nervous I felt to be starting school."

Rob chuckled as he flipped through the pages. There was Susan—a perky third grader with mischief in her eyes. An awkward preteen who looked like she would have paid any price to avoid having her school photo taken while she sported a pimple on her nose. A spunky athlete posing proudly with her junior high basketball team. A happy high school graduate proudly holding her diploma. A grownup-looking young woman dressed in a lavender gown—a bridesmaid at her friend's wedding.

"Okay, which picture is your favorite?" Susan asked playfully when they came to the end of the album.

Turning back toward the front of the book, Rob replied, "This one."

The photo showed Susan as a little girl—perhaps just six or seven years old. She was wearing a bright yellow tee-shirt and faded blue jeans with a bit of grass stain on her right knee. In her hands she was carrying a bouquet of dandelions and clover. Her dad's white handkerchief was draped over her head.

"My 'bridal veil,'" Susan grinned.

"You were pretending to be a bride, weren't you?"

"Yes." She snuggled under Rob's arm. "And now in just a few more days, it'll be for real."

*Take the time to **TALK** about this topic on the next page.*

Thank God—"God, through the years you have watched over me and prepared me to marry the person I love."

Ask God—"Let me never take for granted the positive things that happened during my childhood, and keep me from being discouraged because of the not-so-happy memories. Show me how to build on the positives as I enter this new chapter of my life."

Listen to God—"O LORD, you have searched me and you know me. . . . You are familiar with all my ways. . . . I praise you because I am fearfully and wonderfully made" (Ps. 139:1,3,14).

Know more of what God wants you to do—God has cared for you and loved you throughout your life. Is there any part of your childhood you still need to discuss with your partner to help him or her understand you better?

Day

26

Day 26

ONE FLESH

*G*od didn't make sex a dirty subject. On the contrary, sex is part of God's good, creative design for mankind. He created male and female in his own image, and in the Garden of Eden Adam and Eve "were both naked, and they felt no shame" (Gen. 1:27; 2:25).

In God's plan, sex is not merely the means of reproduction. It is an enjoyable expression of physical, emotional, and spiritual unity, commitment, and love between a husband and wife. It is the union of two bodies, but it is also far more. The Bible even uses marital intimacy to picture the holy love of Christ for his church (Eph. 5:31,32).

In a marriage each person's body belongs not only to himself or herself but also to the spouse. Furthermore, the Bible advises, "Do not deprive each other except by mutual consent and for a time, so that you may devote yourselves to prayer. Then come together again so that Satan will not tempt you because of your lack of self-control" (1 Cor. 7:5).

In *Romeo and Juliet*, Shakespeare wrote, "Love is a smoke rais'd with the fume of sighs . . . a fire sparkling in a lover's eyes." Sexual passion creates warmth and sizzle in a marriage. But like a fire, it can cause great damage if it blazes out of control or burns something it wasn't intended to touch. So once you're married, keep the flames of passion alive. But guard your hearts carefully, stay faithful to each other, and keep the fire within the boundaries God has set—so no one gets burned.

*Take the time to **TALK** about this topic on the next page.*

Thank God—"Thank you for the gift of our love, and a physical way to express our fondness for each other."

Ask God—"Help us to meet each other's needs, to be sexually pure in our attitudes and actions, and to be completely faithful to each other."

Listen to God—"Marriage should be honored by all, and the marriage bed kept pure, for God will judge the adulterer and all the sexually immoral" (Heb. 13:4).

Know more about what God wants you to do— Have you talked openly with your spouse about sexual intimacy? What sexual adjustments do you anticipate during your early years of marriage?

Day

27

~❀ Day 27 ❀~

PARTNERHOOD AND PARENTHOOD

$\mathcal{D}$r. James Dobson tells about the time he was boarding a bus when he saw a woman getting onto the bus with seven children. The woman looked stressed, so he tried to lighten things up with a question.

"Are those kids all yours," he asked, "or is this some kind of picnic?"

"Yes, they're all mine," she answered wearily, "and believe me, it's no picnic!"

In some ways, having children will change your life even more than getting married. If you become parents, you will experience one of life's greatest joys—and you will have less freedom, more responsibility, less privacy, bigger expenses, and more stuff to load into your car. Parenthood will definitely have a profound effect on your "partnerhood."

And parenthood is a sacred trust. Some of the most influential lessons your children will ever learn about life, faith, or marriage, will come from you and your example. Before a married couple has children, it's wise to pray about parenthood and talk about issues like these:

❋ "How many children do we plan to have—and when?"

❋ "How will we plan to nurture, encourage, correct, and discipline our children?"

❋ "What roots (basic, foundational family values) do we want to instill in our children? How will we plan to give them wings (freedom and independence when they're ready to be on their own)?"

❋ "How will we nurture our marriage so that our relationship will be strong after the children are grown and gone from our home?"

*Take the time to **TALK** about this topic on the next page.*

T_hank God_—"I'm grateful for the possibility that we can have a positive influence on the next generation, either by having children of our own or by giving time and attention to the children of others."

A_sk God_—"If you bless our home with children, Lord, help us to be the best parents we can be—and keep our marriage strong in the process."

L_isten to God_—"Your wife will be like a fruitful vine within your house; your sons will be like olive shoots around your table" (Ps. 128:3).

K_now more about what God wants you to do_—Think about how having children might affect your marriage. What changes, adjustments, problems, and joys might result from becoming parents as well as partners?

Day

28

Day 28

IF YOUR MARRIAGE ISN'T PERFECT

*R*obert Frost wrote, "Home is the place where, if you have to go there, they have to take you in." Humorist Tom Mullen added a postscript. He said, "Actually, home is the place where, if you live there, something always has to be fixed!"

All of our homes are imperfect. The Bible says "all have sinned and fall short of the glory of God" (Rom. 3:23). So every marriage inevitably brings together two sinners! We all have weaknesses and imperfections that make it hard for us to relate in a healthy way to others. Some of us carry deep-seated hurts—wounds we've received when others have mistreated us in the past.

If your marriage isn't perfect, you're normal! How can two imperfect people have a perfect marriage? They can't! But you can still have an excellent and fulfilling marriage, a lasting and satisfying marriage, if you . . .

* Personally accept the free gift of God's grace through Jesus Christ—a gift that makes up for all the wrongs you have done.

* Extend lots of grace to your mate—forgiving wrongs, refusing to hold grudges, resolving con-

flicts quickly, accepting that he/she has faults that you can't change.

❋ Honestly acknowledge your sins and shortcomings to God and to your spouse.

Be patient with each other—one sinner to another. With God's help, your home can be a hospital where imperfect people find acceptance and healing.

Take the time to **TALK** *about this topic on the next page.*

Thank God—"Thank you, God, for loving me even when I act unlovable."

Ask God—"Let us see past each other's imperfections and accept each other with lots of grace and mercy."

Listen to God—"Bear with each other and forgive whatever grievances you may have against one another. Forgive as the Lord forgave you" (Col. 3:13).

Know more about what God wants you to do—One definition of grace is "undeserved favor or kindness." How will you demonstrate grace to your mate today?

Day

29

❧ Day 29 ❧
I CHOOSE YOU

*L*ife is filled with choices. Paper or plastic? Cash or credit? Regular or decaf? Chocolate or vanilla?

In marriage, simple decisions sometimes become sources of irritation and even heated debate. Which way should the toilet paper unroll—forward or backward? Should we squeeze the toothpaste tube from the bottom up, or mash it right in the middle? Who will sleep on which side of the bed? What will we eat for dinner, and when?

Big decisions are even harder. Where should we live? Can we afford to buy a house? Should we consider changing careers? What about having children?

We need to keep our choices in perspective. Jesus spoke about what our priorities should be when he said, "Seek first [God's] kingdom and his righteousness, and all these things will be given to you as well" (Matt. 6:33). Next to deciding to put God first in our lives, the choice of a mate is one of the most important other decisions we'll ever make. In marriage, two people say to each other . . .

❋ "My love for you is freely given as an act of my will."

❀ "It's noble to remain single and I could have chosen to do so, but I'm glad I have decided to spend my life with you."

❀ "My love for you is reliable. I will choose to give myself to you even during times when responsibility seems to outweigh romance, when fickle feelings waver, when temptations lure me to question my relationship with you. I'll still be there. That's my commitment, my choice."

❀ "Out of all the people in the world, I choose you. And I'm glad you've chosen me too!"

Take the time to **TALK** *about this topic on the next page.*

T*hank God*—"God, it feels good to be wanted. Thank you for my spouse, and the choice we have made to be together."

A*sk God*—"Give us strength to fulfill the promises we have made to each other."

L*isten to God*—"[Love] burns like blazing fire, like a mighty flame. Many waters cannot quench love; rivers cannot wash it away" (S of S. 8:6b,7a).

K*now more about what God wants you to do*— Life isn't just about what happens to us. It's about the choices we make, and how we respond to our circumstances. Think about the three biggest decisions you've ever made. How will your decision to get married affect the direction of your life?

Day

30

~ Day 30 ~

IT'S NOT AUTOMATIC

*M*y daughter Melinda does fine in her college classes, but recently she faced a new educational challenge: learning to drive a car with a manual transmission.

She doesn't like it when I say, "You've been spoiled by automatic transmissions. Now you're really going to learn how to drive."

Nor does she like it when she drives down the street with a series of jerks and jolts. "What if I come to a stoplight at the top of a big hill," she worries, "and start to roll backward when I try to shift gears? And what if that happens while another car is directly behind me?"

"That's part of the excitement," I tell her. A manual transmission gets more body parts involved: left foot on the clutch, right hand on the gearshift knob, left hand steering the car. "Think of it as exercise," I say. "You'll burn more calories driving that way." Melinda is not amused.

To be honest, though, sometimes I prefer to function on automatic, too—even in my marriage. After many years together, Candy and I automatically understand a lot of things about each other. She knows instantly when

I'm feeling restless or bored. (She says I fidget and my leg jiggles up and down.) Instinctively, I know how long she needs to comb her hair and freshen her makeup before we go out for the evening. (I've spent a lot of time waiting with my leg jiggling.) We know many mindless details about each other: favorite salad dressings, TV shows we detest, pet peeves, and silly habits. It's tempting to slip into autopilot and take each other for granted.

The Greek word *automatos* means "self-acting." When I put my marriage on automatic, I end up acting mainly for myself. Love, though, "is not self-seeking" (1 Cor. 13:5).

Like driving a car with a manual transmission, it takes a little more effort to build adventure and intimacy into a marriage. Sometimes you grind the gears a bit, but that's okay as long as you keep moving forward. A good marriage doesn't happen automatically. Without intentional acts of kindness, without some deliberate moments of spontaneity, without deciding to pursue some new adventures, a relationship will slide backward like a poorly driven car at a stoplight on top of a hill.

Familiarity doesn't have to breed contempt. It can actually breed contentment, security, and deeper joy. That's the direction I want my marriage to go—even if it means I have to shift some gears now and then.

Take the time to **TALK** *about this topic on the next page.*

Thank God—"Father, we're grateful for the things that are predictable about our relationship, and for the surprising discoveries we continue to make as we grow together."

Ask God—"Help us not to be selfish or to take one another for granted. Refresh and renew us so that our marriage never grows stale, but grows stronger and deeper with the passing of time."

Listen to God—"Each of you should look not only to your own interests, but also to the interests of others" (Phil. 2:4).

Know more about what God wants you to do— Discuss with your partner: What is predictable and "automatic" about your relationship? How often do you try something new and spontaneous? How can you keep your relationship fresh and exciting?

Day

31

🌺 Day 31 🌺

TILL DEATH DO US PART

*M*y dad and I were traveling together, and our plane stopped in Knoxville, Tennessee, for a short stop before we headed home to Cincinnati, Ohio. The flight to Cincinnati was overbooked, so the airline began to offer incentives to passengers willing to give up their seats. When they offered us a free night in a hotel, a flight out the next morning, plus a free round-trip ticket for a future flight, I was ready to volunteer.

"Dad, let's stay one extra night," I told him.

But Dad hesitated.

"Come on, we'll still be home by midday tomorrow," I insisted. I couldn't understand why he would balk at such a good offer.

Finally Dad explained why he didn't want to delay getting home. "Tomorrow is my wedding anniversary," he said, "and I want to spend the entire day with your mother."

Dad and Mom got married in 1946. After more than 50 years of marriage, they still want to be together any chance they get. I want that kind of marriage

myself—don't you? The kind that lasts, and loves, for a lifetime.

We took the early flight home.

Take the time to **TALK** *about this topic on the next page.*

Thank God—"Thank you for couples who have been happily married for many years. Their faithfulness encourages me and gives me confidence that our marriage will be successful too."

Ask God—"Please give us a strong bond of love that lasts for a lifetime."

Listen to God—"May you rejoice in the wife of your youth. . . . May you ever be captivated by her love" (Prov. 5:18,19).

Know more about what God wants you to do—Based on what you already know about your partner, what do you think he or she will be like ten years from now? Fifty years from now? What do you think you will be like? Ponder the kind of people you hope to be as you and your spouse grow older together.